CW01217024

kevin
mayhew

First published in Great Britain in 2019 by Kevin Mayhew Ltd
Buxhall, Stowmarket, Suffolk IP14 3BW
Tel: +44 (0) 1449 737978 Fax: +44 (0) 1449 737834
E-mail: info@kevinmayhew.com

www.kevinmayhew.com

© Copyright 2019 Graham Jeffery

The right of Graham Jeffery to be identified as the author of this work has been asserted by him in accordance with the Copyright, Designs and Patents Act 1988. The publishers wish to thank all those who have given their permission to reproduce copyright material in this publication.

Scripture quotations are taken from The Holy Bible, New International Version® Anglicised, NIV®, copyright © 1979, 1984, 2011 by Biblica Inc.®. Used by permission. All rights reserved worldwide.

All rights reserved. No part of this publication may be reproduced, stored in a retrieval system, or transmitted, in any form or by any means, electronic, mechanical, photocopying, recording, or otherwise, without the prior written permission of the publisher.

9 8 7 6 5 4 3 2 1 0

ISBN 978 1 83858 034 6
Catalogue No. 1501628

Cover design and layout by Rob Mortonson
Dear Dog illustrations by Graham Jeffery
Printed and bound in Hong Kong

Graham Jeffery

Dear Dog

A little dog's guide
to the gospel

**kevin
mayhew**

Graham Jeffery was ordained in 1960 at Winchester Cathedral and recently retired after serving a small parish in Sussex for 32 years.

He is more used to writing prayers for grown-ups and children, and the bishop's last words to him (in 1961) were 'keep drawing'.

Dear Dog

Dear Dog,
I know you are
God spelt backwards
but there is
nothing backward
in your care
of me.

You may not have
come down
from heaven,
but you help me
to go up.

Not suddenly, but by little
steps you help me.
So many little journeys
making one great journey;
my whole life, in fact.

I only ever make one journey.

Every walk, however little,
is part of the journey.

And God said . . .

. . . let there be Labradors.

You chose me.

Jesus didn't choose
his 12 disciples
at 'Crufts'.

But how did you
know it was me
you were looking for?

I'd rather be
a failed mongrel
than a successful
Rottweiler.

Keep me as the apple
of your eye;
hide me in the
shadow of your wings.

Psalm 17:8

Small disciples give the greatest praise.

But it's not easy
to follow you,
Jesus . . .

I would follow you today, Jesus, but I'm rather tied up.

It's not easy following in Jesus' footsteps when he keeps going by boat.

Show me your ways, Lord,
teach me your paths.

Guide me in your truth
and teach me, for you
are God my Saviour,
and my hope is in you
all day long.

Psalm 25:4, 5

I'm 100% behind you, Jesus.

Perhaps I'd better make that 97.3%.

A Labrador and his walk are not easily parted.

You call us to do
life together with others
that are often
so different from us . . .

We don't always get to choose our fellow disciples.

We find our allies in the most unexpected places.

Some people take all the advantage they can get.

Now you are
the body of Christ,
and each one of you
is a part of it.

1 Corinthians 12:27

I sometimes think Christianity is more suitable for cats.

Call it a marriage of convenience.

I've never known
seven days pass
so slowly.

Even best friends go at different speeds.

Glad to see Moses got something right.

We all follow Jesus
in our different ways.

We have different gifts,
according to the grace given
to each of us.
If your gift is prophesying,
then prophesy in accordance
with your faith; if it is serving,
then serve; if it is teaching,
then teach; if it is to encourage,
then give encouragement;
if it is giving, then give
generously; if it is to lead,
do it diligently; if it is to show
mercy, do it cheerfully.

Romans 12:6-8

We all have our
communication problems.

Accept one another,
then, just as Christ
accepted you,
in order to
bring praise to God.

Romans 15:7

All Welcome

provided you are
politically correct
sexually stable
financially secure
religiously sound

At least Jesus got to write the first two words.

Sometimes, Jesus,
I think I know best . . .

The fact I don't bark at something doesn't mean that I approve of it.

Coming Jesus, but can I chase this cat first?

I'd be a saint
if it wasn't
for my bark.

I choose my owners
very carefully.

I never let go
of a problem
till it is properly
digested.

I still think
it would have been
quicker by air.

Either this wallpaper goes or I do.

If this isn't heaven,
what is?

It's not smooth sailing.

Life is still full of ups and downs, laughter and tears . . .

Staying still is not always an option.

Suppose one of you has a hundred sheep and loses one of them. Doesn't he leave the ninety-nine in the open country and go after the lost sheep until he finds it?

Luke 15:4

Christianity is a religion to die for.

If Jesus can't climb up to rescue it, nobody can.

Along the way you constantly remind me that I am loved . . .

I'd know those footprints anywhere.

Being small doesn't mean you are a minor character.

I know who's at
the end of my lead.

Whatever part of the sky you're in, you can always shine.

Those who are wise
will shine like the
brightness of the heavens,
and those who lead
many to righteousness,
like the stars
for ever and ever.

Daniel 12:3

You know what I want,
before I ask.

Now to him who is able
to do immeasurably more
than all we ask or imagine,
according to his power
that is at work within us,
to him be glory in the church
and in Christ Jesus
throughout all generations,
for ever and ever!
Amen.

Ephesians 3:20, 21

You give me other worlds to walk in.

I'd rather be lost with you
than found with anyone else.

No friends

No Power

No Influence

No Reputation

No Money

With a failure like this, who needs success?

It's not the journey
that matters . . .

only who comes with you.

Here am I,
send me.

In your eyes, Lord,
I never get older.

It's just that I've spent
longer in your company.

And when you can't
see the star,
keep a lookout
for the shepherd.

Sheep may safely gaze

And then again, mathematics was never his strong point.

And I will dwell in your heart forever.

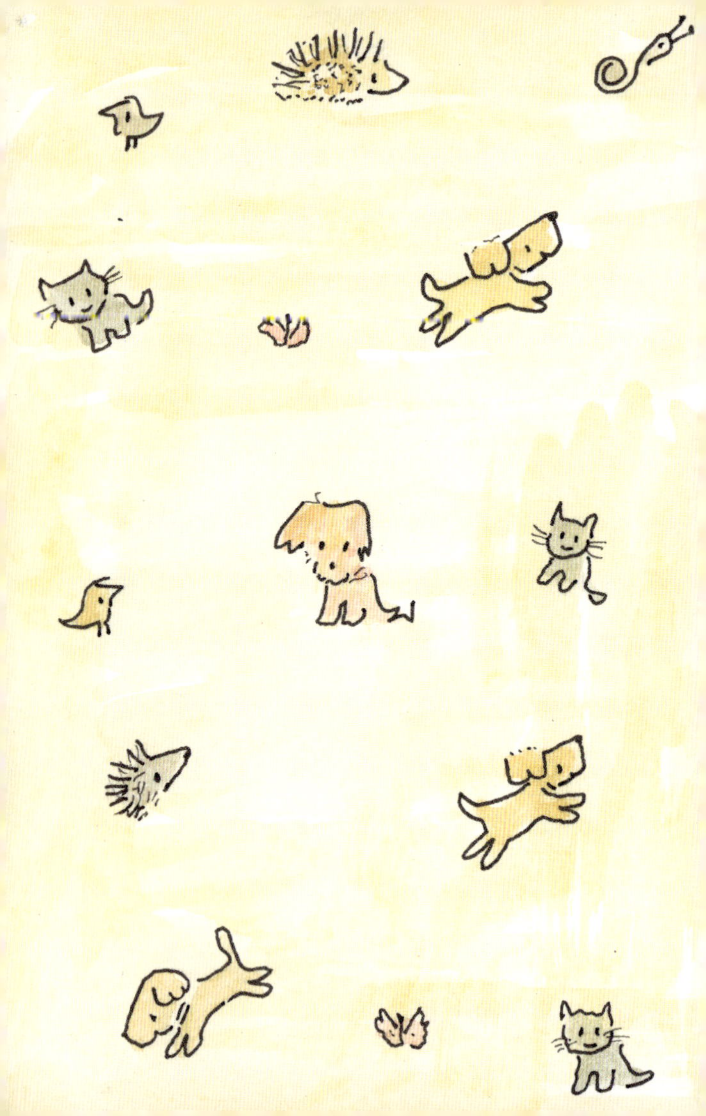